Hazel's fire safety adventures

BOOK-2

MEET HAZEL. SHE IS EXCITED TO GO ON AN ADVENTURE AND TEACH YOU ABOUT FIRE SAFETY!

HI! MY NAME IS HAZEL, AND I WANT
TO TEACH YOU ABOUT STAYING SAFE
WHEN THERE IS A FIRE.
LET'S WEAR OUR SAFETY HELMETS
AND HEAD TO THE FIRE STATION.

AT THE FIRE STATION, HAZEL MEETS
FIREFIGHTER MIKE, WHO TEACHES HER
ABOUT THE IMPORTANCE OF SMOKE
DETECTORS.

HAZEL LEARNS HOW TO STOP, DROP, AND ROLL IF HER CLOTHES EVER CATCH ON FIRE. SHE PRACTICES WITH FIREFIGHTER MIKE AND FEELS PROUD OF HERSELF.

FIREFIGHTER MIKE TEACHES HAZEL HOW TO CALL AN EMERGENCY SERVICE IN CASE OF AN EMERGENCY. SHE LEARNS TO GIVE HER NAME, ADDRESS, AND THE TYPE OF EMERGENCY.

HAZEL VISITS THE FIRE STATION'S KITCHEN AND LEARNS HOW TO USE A FIRE EXTINGUISHER TO PUT OUT A SMALL FIRE.

HAZEL LEARNS THAT WE SHOULD NOT LEAVE CANDLES AND INCENSE UNATTENDED. ALWAYS EXTINGUISH THEM BEFORE LEAVING THE ROOM.

HAZEL LEARNS THAT MATCHES AND LIGHTERS ARE NOT TOYS AND SHOULD ONLY BE USED BY GROWN-UPS. SHE MAKES A PROMISE TO NEVER PLAY WITH THEM.

FIRES CAN START IN THE KITCHEN. IT IS VERY IMPORTANT TO ALWAYS HAVE AN ADULT WITH YOU WHEN YOU ARE COOKING.

FIREPLACES CAN BE COZY AND WARM, BUT THEY CAN ALSO BE DANGEROUS. ALWAYS MAKE SURE THAT YOU HAVE A GROWN-UP AROUND WHEN THERE'S A FIRE IN THE FIREPLACE.

CAMPFIRES CAN BE FUN, BUT THEY CAN ALSO BE DANGEROUS. ALWAYS MAKE SURE THAT YOU HAVE A GROWN-UP AROUND WHEN YOU'RE NEAR A CAMPFIRE.

ELECTRICAL FIRES CAN START WHEN THERE ARE TOO MANY THINGS PLUGGED INTO AN OUTLET. ALWAYS MAKE SURE THAT YOU'RE NOT OVERLOADING YOUR OUTLETS.

SMOKE ALARMS ARE VERY IMPORTANT BECAUSE THEY CAN ALERT YOU TO A FIRE BEFORE IT'S TOO LATE. MAKE SURE THAT YOU HAVE A SMOKE ALARM IN EVERY BEDROOM AND ON EVERY FLOOR OF YOUR HOUSE.

HAZEL LEARNS THAT IF THERE IS A FIRE, GET OUT OF THE HOUSE AS QUICKLY AS POSSIBLE AND CALL FOR HELP.

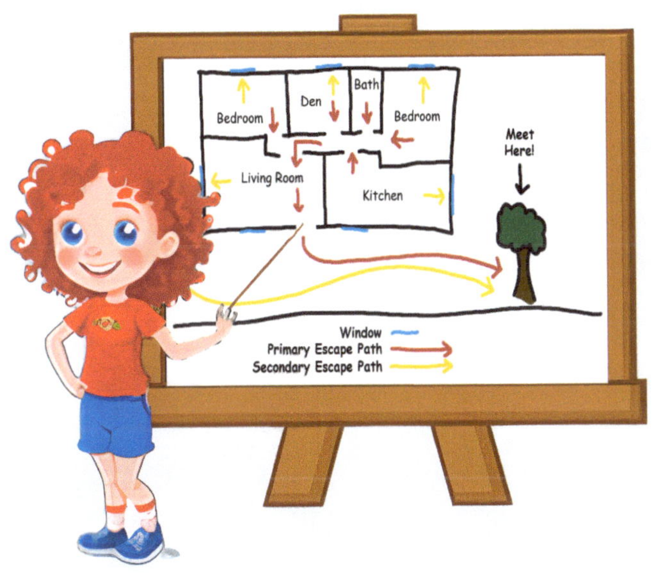

HAZEL AND HER FAMILY PRACTICE THEIR FIRE ESCAPE PLAN TOGETHER. THEY MAKE SURE THAT EVERYONE KNOWS WHAT TO DO IN CASE OF A FIRE.

DURING AN EMERGENCY, AVOID USING AN ELEVATOR. ALWAYS USE THE STAIRS WHILE EXITING THE BUILDING.

LET'S TAKE A QUIZ TO SEE IF YOU
REMEMBER WHAT WE LEARNED
ABOUT FIRE SAFETY.

WHEN YOU CALL ANY EMERGENCY SERVICE, WHAT INFORMATION WOULD YOU GIVE THEM?

Name: ______________________________

Adress: ______________________________

Type of emergency: ______________________________

WHAT DO YOU DO IF YOUR CLOTHES ARE ON FIRE?

WHAT DO YOU USE TO PUT OUT A SMALL FIRE?

GET READY FOR OUR NEXT ADVENTURE AS HAZEL TEACHES US THE IMPORTANCE OF PERSONAL HYGIENE FOR STAYING HEALTHY AND HAPPY!